Reading with Ricky
Butterflies, Woodpeckers, and Bears

Stories by Kathy Kranking
Illustrations by Christian Slade

Contents

Hello, Butterfly!

It was a bright, sunny day. Ricky Raccoon was watering his butterfly garden—a special garden filled with flowers that butterflies like. As butterflies fluttered around Ricky, Bizzie Beaver came walking up.

"Hi, Ricky," said Bizzie. "Wow! Look at all the butterflies!"

As Ricky and Bizzie watched, a butterfly landed on a nearby flower. It uncurled its long tongue and poked it into the center of the flower.

"It's drinking nectar!" said Ricky.

After a minute or two, the butterfly flew off the flower and fluttered around Ricky and Bizzie. It came so close to Ricky that he thought it was going to land on him. Then it flew away.

"I have an idea," Ricky said to Bizzie. "I want to get a butterfly to land on me!"

"Really?" asked Bizzie. "How are you going to do that?"

FLORA WANTS TO KNOW

Do you think a butterfly will land on Ricky?

“Well,” said Ricky, “maybe if I just sit really still for a long time, a butterfly will land on me.”

“I want to try, too!” said Bizzie excitedly.

Ricky and Bizzie sat on the garden bench. They sat very still. A minute went by. Then another. Bizzie began to feel squirmy. Butterflies were on the flowers all around them. All of a sudden, Bizzie’s nose felt tickly. *“AHCHOO!”* he sneezed. The startled butterflies flew off the flowers.

“I’m sorry,” Bizzie said. “I’m not very good at sitting still.”

“It’s OK,” said Ricky. “I’m going to keep trying.” So Bizzie went home and Ricky kept sitting quietly on the bench. But even after more than an hour, no butterflies had landed on him.

“Oh, well,” he said to himself. “I’ll try again tomorrow.”

The next day, Flora Skunk headed over to Ricky’s house. When she got there, she saw a strange sight. Ricky was sitting on his garden bench. And he was covered in flowers! Flowers were on his cap and around his neck. And he was holding a small bouquet in each of his paws.

BIZZIE WONDERS

Are you good at sitting still and being quiet?

"Hi, Ricky," Flora said. "Why are you covered in flowers?"

"I'm trying to get a butterfly to land on me," Ricky answered quietly. "I figured if I covered myself in flowers, they might think I was a flower, too."

"That makes sense," said Flora. She noticed a camera next to Ricky.

"What's the camera for?" she asked.

"If a butterfly lands on me, I want to take a picture to hang in my house," said Ricky.

"Cool," Flora said. "I'll come back tomorrow to see if it worked."

Flora headed off, and Ricky continued to sit quietly. A few times, a butterfly landed on the flowers he was holding. But none landed right on him.

The next day, Flora ran into Bizzie as she was heading over to visit Ricky.

"I'm going to Ricky's to find out if he got a butterfly to land on him," Bizzie said.

“That’s what I’m doing, too,” said Flora.

As Flora and Bizzie came around a bend they could see Ricky’s garden. And there was Ricky, sitting on the bench. But as they got closer, they could see that Ricky had dropped the flowers he was holding. His head was back, and his cap had fallen off.

“Ricky’s sound asleep!” said Flora.

“He must have been sitting there for a long time!” Bizzie said.

Flora and Bizzie walked up to Ricky. Butterflies were fluttering around the flowers as Ricky snoozed away. Then, all of a sudden, one of the butterflies flew close to Ricky. It circled slowly around his head a few times. Then it landed on his nose!

“Should we wake Ricky up?” Bizzie asked.

“No,” said Flora. “Ricky would move and scare off the butterfly.” Then she saw the camera on the bench. “I have an idea!” she said. “We’ll take a picture. Then we can frame it and give it to Ricky to hang in his house!”

And that’s exactly what they did!

RICKY ASKS

Would you like a butterfly to land on your nose?

LEARN MORE

Butterfly Bodies

A butterfly's wings are covered with tiny scales. The scales give the wings their color.

A butterfly smells with its two antennas (an-TEN-uhz).

A butterfly drinks through a long, hollow tube called a proboscis (pro-BAH-sis).

Hooray for Holes

It was a cool fall day in Deep Green Wood. The ground was covered with a carpet of leaves.

"Woo-hoo!" shouted Ricky Raccoon as he flew through the air. A second later, he landed in a big leaf pile with a *whoosh!*

"Awesome!" Ricky said, as he popped out of the pile. A few leaves were stuck to his head.

Ricky, Bizzie Beaver, Flora Skunk, and Sammy Skunk had been playing in the leaves all morning. Now, as they sat down to rest, Ricky noticed something. "Hey gang, I see something cool," he said. "Come on!"

The others followed Ricky as he ran. He stopped in front of a huge tree, and everyone gathered around it, staring.

"Wow!" said Flora.

It was an old, dead tree. But the unusual thing about it was the big hole at the base of the trunk.

BIZZIE WANTS TO KNOW

What's your favorite thing to do in the fall?

"That hole is big enough for me to fit inside," said Sammy. He crawled into the hole and sat down with a grin.

"We could use this tree as a soccer tree!" said Ricky.

"What's a soccer tree?" asked Bizzie.

Ricky smiled. "It's a tree that has a soccer goal!" he said, pointing to the big hole.

"Oh, I get it," said Flora. "That's a really fun idea!"

The friends decided to go home for lunch, then return afterward with Ricky's soccer ball so they could play.

Later on, they were all back at the tree with full tummies and a black-and-white ball.

"I don't know how to play soccer," said Sammy.

"Don't worry," said Ricky. "It's easy. We'll break up into teams—you and Flora against Bizzie and me. Each team works together to kick the ball into the goal—I mean, tree hole. And each team also tries to keep the other from kicking the ball into the hole."

FLORA WONDERS

Have you ever played soccer?

Flora and Sammy had the ball first. Flora kicked the ball past Ricky to Sammy. Then Sammy tried to kick the ball into the tree-hole goal. But Bizzie blocked it from going in.

“Better luck next time!” Bizzie said.

Bizzie kicked the ball toward Ricky. But Sammy ran up and kicked the ball before Ricky could get to it. The ball sailed right past Bizzie as he tried to block it. And into the hole it went!

“Gooooaaaaaaal!” shouted Ricky, as Flora high-fived Sammy.

“I did it! I did it!” said Sammy.

The teams started playing again. This time Ricky tried to make a goal. But Flora kicked the ball away. The ball went flying over the others’ heads.

“I’ll get it,” Ricky said, chasing after the ball. He ran to where the ball had landed. But as Ricky was about to pick it up, something black and white flapped past his head. It was a big, flashy bird. But it disappeared before Ricky could get a really good look at it.

Ricky grabbed the ball and ran back to his friends.

"I saw the coolest thing!" he said. "It was black and white, and it flew right past me."

"The soccer ball?" asked Sammy.

Ricky laughed. "No, I saw a really big bird. And there it is!" Ricky pointed as the black-and-white bird landed on the soccer tree. He saw now that it had a red crest on its head.

As the gang watched, the bird began pecking at the tree trunk with its bill. It made a loud *knock! knock!* noise as it pecked.

"It's a woodpecker!" said Flora.

"I remember Mrs. Cardinal telling us that woodpeckers peck holes in dead trees to find insects to eat," said Bizzie.

"For us, this is a soccer tree," said Ricky. "But for that bird, it's a *knocker* tree!"

RICKY ASKS

How is a woodpecker like a soccer ball?

LEARN MORE

WOODPECKERS

Woodpeckers **knock-knock-knock** on wood all day long. They do it to find food, make nest holes, and talk to other woodpeckers.

RAT-A-TAT-TAT!

The bird's bill is big, sharp, and super tough.

A thick, spongy skull protects the bird's brain from getting knocked around.

Stiff tail feathers support the bird as it hammers.

Bird Feeder Mystery

Ricky Raccoon was sitting on the bench outside his house. He had a big smile on his face. That's because watching the birds at his feeder was one of his favorite things! Cardinals, sparrows, blue jays, chickadees, and lots of other birds were flying down from the trees to gobble up yummy seed.

"Hi, Ricky! What are you doing?" he heard someone say.

Ricky turned to see his friend Bizzie Beaver walking up with Flora Skunk and Mitzi Mink.

"I was just watching my favorite show," said Ricky.

Ricky's friends looked puzzled.

"Show?" asked Flora.

"But where's your TV?" asked Bizzie.

Ricky laughed. "I don't mean a TV show," he said. "I mean this show." He pointed at the feeder.

"Look at all the birds!" said Mitzi.

"Cool!" Flora said. "The bird feeder is like a busy restaurant."

The friends sat and watched until most of the birds were gone.

"That was fun," said Bizzie. "Maybe we'll come back tomorrow to watch with you again."

The next morning, Ricky headed outside with a cup of hot cocoa to watch his bird friends eat their breakfast. But he got a surprise. The feeder was gone!

“I wonder what happened to the feeder?” thought Ricky.

Just then, the gang showed up. “We came back to watch the birds,” Flora said.

“The bird feeder has disappeared!” said Ricky.

Ricky’s friends looked over at where the feeder had been. “Wow, those birds must have been really hungry,” said Bizzie.

“Bizzie, don’t be silly,” said Mitzi. “The birds could not have eaten the whole feeder. Something else must have happened to it.”

“Let’s look around,” said Flora. “Maybe we can find it.”

The friends spread out and began hunting for the missing bird feeder. After a few minutes, Ricky shouted, “I found it!”

Flora, Mitzi, and Bizzie ran over to where Ricky was. And sure enough, the feeder was on the ground. Some seed had spilled out of it, but otherwise it seemed OK.

"Why would someone move the feeder?" asked Ricky. Then he picked it up and hung it back in the tree where it had been.

"It's a mystery," said Bizzie.

Soon the birds began coming to the feeder and gobbling up seed. All seemed to be back to normal.

BIZZIE ASKS

Who do you think moved the bird feeder?

But very early the next morning, some noises woke Ricky up. “What’s that?” he asked himself sleepily. He got up and looked out the window. And Ricky could hardly believe what he saw.

The feeder was on the ground again. And next to it was a bear! The bear was pawing at the feeder and eating the bird seed that fell from it.

“Holy cow!” said Ricky. “I mean, holy bear,” he added with a little giggle.

Ricky watched as the bear wrestled with the feeder, dragging it along the ground and pawing at it to get more seed out.

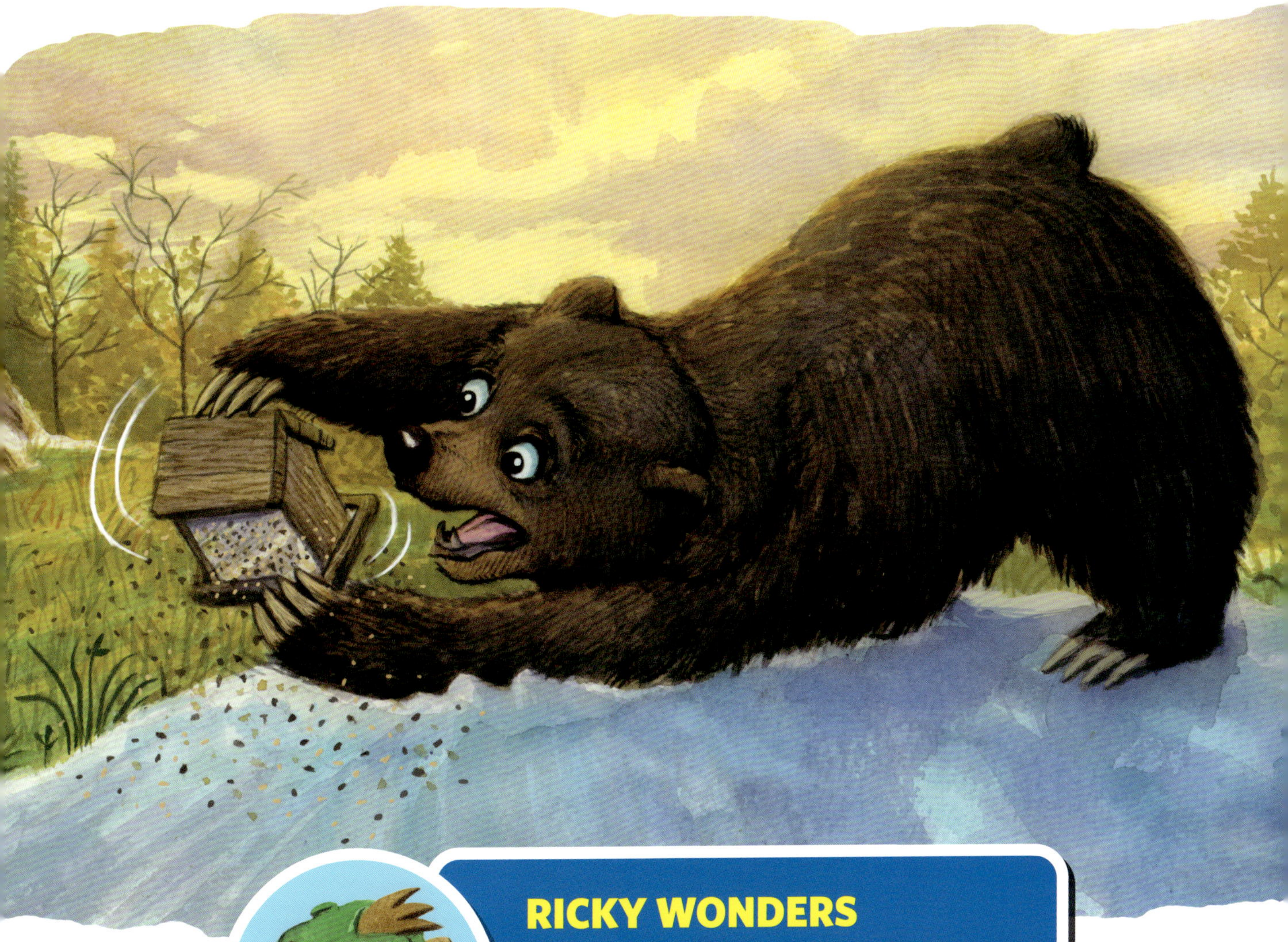

RICKY WONDERS

Why would a bear want to eat bird seed?

"No wonder the feeder was so far away from the tree yesterday," Ricky thought. "That bear wants to take it home!"

Ricky watched the bear for a long time, until finally it lumbered off into the woods. Then he went out to hang the feeder back up. Just as he was doing that, Flora, Bizzie, and Mitzi arrived.

"Was the feeder on the ground again?" asked Flora.

"Did you figure out what happened?" added Bizzie.

Ricky grinned. "It was, and I did," he said. Then he told them about the bear.

"Wow!" his friends all said at the exact same time.

"The other day, Flora said the bird feeder was like a restaurant," Ricky said. "Little did we know that a bear would be one of the customers!"

FLORA WANTS TO KNOW

Do you know what else bears eat?

LEARN MORE

HUNGRY AS A BEAR

GRIZZLY BEAR
My favorite food is fish.

PANDA BEAR
The only thing I eat is bamboo.

BLACK BEAR
I'm not picky. I'll eat anything I can find.

Published by the National Wildlife Federation.

"Ricky and Pals" originally appeared in Ranger Rick Jr, a publication for children ages 4–7 in the Ranger Rick family of magazines.

Kathy Kranking, Author
Christian Slade, Illustrator
Molly Woods, Reading Consultant

Photo and Illustration Credits:
Pages 10–11: Richard Day / Daybreak Images; Steve Gettle / Minden Pictures (inset); Page 20: Todd Kiraly / T-Minus Ten Designs; Page 21: Gary Davenport; Page 30: Sean Crane / Minden Pictures; Page 31: Josef Gelernter (top), Donald M. Jones / Minden Pictures (bottom).

Printed in the United States of America.

RangerRick.org

ISBN: 978-1-947254-30-5